FORT WORTH PUBLIC LIBRARY

3 1668 03732 3125

SO-BEG-381

Are We There Yet?

811.54 JONES 2008
Jones, Roger
Are we there yet?

Central   04/28/2010

CENTRAL LIBRARY

Are We There Yet?

Roger Jones

Texas Review Press
Huntsville, Texas

FORT WORTH LIBRARY

Copyright © 2008 by Roger Jones
All rights reserved
Printed in the United States of America

FIRST EDITION, 2008
Requests for permission to reproduce material from this work should be sent
to:

    Permissions
    Texas Review Press
    English Department
    Sam Houston State University
    Huntsville, TX 77341-2146

Acknowledgments:

Grateful acknowledgment is made to the editors of the following journals, in
which some of the poems in this collection first appeared:

*Arkansas Review, Baltimore Review, Blue Unicorn, Borderlands, California
Quarterly, Ceteris Paribus, Cimarron Review, Concho River Review, Crab Creek
Review, Danforth Review, DeKalb Literary Arts Journal, Descant* (TCU),
*Evansville Review, Grasslands Review, Hampden-Sydney Poetry Journal, Hawaii
Pacific Review, Janus Head, Louisiana Literature, New Jersey Poetry Journal,
Oklahoma Review, Old Hickory Review, Poem, Red River Review, Rio Grande
Review, Sierra Nevada College Review, Southern Poetry Review, Texas Observer,
Texas Review, 2 Rivers,* and *Wolf Head Quarterly.*

"Arrivals," which first appeared in *Texas Review,* was reprinted in *Anthology of
Magazine Verse and Yearbook of American Poetry* (1996)

Library of Congress Cataloging-in-Publication Data

Jones, Roger, 1954-
  Are we there yet? / Roger Jones. -- 1st ed.
    p. cm.
  ISBN-13: 978-1-933896-05-2 (pbk. : alk. paper)
  ISBN-10: 1-933896-05-1 (pbk. : alk. paper)
  1. Travel--Poetry. 2. Time--Poetry. 3. Life--Poetry. I. Title.
  PS3560.O5266A88 2007
  811'.54--dc22

                2007023580

To Rene, Colin and Chloe
and our parents and family.

CONTENTS

I.

II.

Are We There Yet?

I

ARRIVALS

for Colin

One night in the airport, my father
watched a star or blip of light become
a blip growing slowly in the east.
Like a magi, standing still
at the window's hold-on rail, he
watched it sink and grow, homing
on this moment, the small
airport, the flattest land on earth,
deep West Texas. Soon
with rubbery shrieks a Boeing 737
set down routinely on the tarmac,
wheeling around to a wheezy stop
at the concourse, at whose gate
he watched the doorway, waiting
until my wife and I emerged
out of the gaggle of tired travelers,
home after a long absence.

I think of his faith that moment
as I stand today in the ghostly dark
of the technician's lab, staring
into a dark tv screen at an image
pulled from pre- or after-life, or drawn
by graphite pencil: the exposed
shadowy winglike span of my wife's
womb, fine net of her bloodwork,
wherein the walnut-sized space
appears, and the doctor taps twice
with his pen on the blinking light:
a heartbeat, first child, son.
I see the future begin there like a needle
pushing itself through the stitch

of where I stand, toward a future
neither my father nor I will see,
but there; and I watch it approach,
and cheer it on, watching it blink
on, off, coming in, coming closer,
coming home for good.

FIRST GRADE

Aftertaste of chocolate milk;
sleek sun dancing off windows;
the small paper clocks
we spent so many days on, fixing hands
with tacks, turning and turning them
to learn the names of the hours—

but none of my classmates' names comes back.
Not the boy with rumpled
black hair in front of me.
Not the girl with pale blue eyes
who raised her hand every question.
Their faces I see clearly,

and the opened door
we longed each day to bolt through,
and the red and yellow cut-out paper leaves
about to blow away on the bulletin board.
But no names return, even if
I stare long into the familiar faces.

And what about the teacher
who stayed only a year in our small town?—
dark-haired, quiet, always sad,
her husband off at war in another land.

Calm and younger in my mind, her face
reflects bronze light from the trees.
She looks up from her desk, about to speak,
to call on me with a question.
And did I know the answer?
And could I tell her now?

CLOVER

On hands and knees I'd shimmy through it
as a child, smearing my jeaned knees
with summer's green light. At ground level
I'd gaze across the baseball field grass
as bees skimmed lightly atop each plumed
clover blossom, the mysterious dance and waggle.
Soon calm white houses fading slowly opened
for voices singing a name up and down the street.
Scrambling up from all-fours, I'd tear out,
hearing my own voice calling back, and race
zig-zagging through dark trees, seizing
like honey any daylight I could take home,
knowing no matter what darkness, I could use it.

CIRCLE OF WATERMELON

I cut a circular slice of watermelon
from the Charleston Grey we picked
from the garden. I placed my slab in a pan
and ate it all, spitting out the seeds
in the mizzling soup (poured out by the door—
a melon vine sprouted there this spring);

I took the hollowed hoop of melon down
to the woods, the pond and fence line
marking the north side of our neighbor's property.
I cut my initials, and the date I ate it
into the melon's crisp rind
and left it looped around a crooked fence post.

I went back this spring to the place and found
no rind, no curled up roiling remnant,
no husk in the high grass, nothing of the green-
pink piece I devoured one sweltering evening,
though I stood thinking back: my initials
carved there, the summer sun
cutting its own name into the flash of my body.

ENLISTMENT

The Great Depression and War loomed
in our house like old relatives—
whispered in the closets,
in the rain creaking quietly
on wooden shingles.

They lived in the dust
that settled on books in our shelves,
in dark that milled our house
late hours when everyone slept.

They were on our hands,
in our skin: quiet, plaintive words,
Never again.

The toys jumbled in the toybox
wore grimness and victory.
Hunger shouted from my clothes:

that little worn suit
clipped by a hanger to a nail;
the shoes I could never keep polished;
the shirts given to me
by someone to whom they'd been given—

these were my uniform,
the body given by those who loved me,
a token each year to tell me
I was theirs, and should be ready
any time, should I be called
to the line.

TIDAL

I'm eating scallops, tiny creatures
I imagine as the innocents of the ocean,
the lowest rank of the food chain except for
kelp and plankton, and tiny plants too small
for human sight. You eat oysters, perfect flesh
coerced from within rocky clumps of shell.
Across the road the ocean beats and batters

the night and sea wall with fists of wind.
From our restaurant window, we find tiny lights
of fishing boats sprinkled out at sea,
where the great wish and wane of the tides
wheels back again. Here we're comfortable,
romantic, our table bedecked with wine,
candles, while waiters whisk back and forth

from the kitchen carrying second helpings
of bread, drink. It's good to take in such
plenitude: the night, the food. Soon we'll go back
to our room, fall together and lie rhythmic,
awash in the brightness of being, brandishing
together through the flash of sleep these delicacies
that flake so warm and light into our mouths.

PRACTICE

Late autumn, the stadium's open, empty.
We walk out between hash marks half-hidden
in frost-seared grass, and run old patterns:
the slant, the curl, the post, the flag.
Lobbing the football back and forth, we feel
familiarity in the touch, the hard lacing
and pebbled leather. Under an early moon

he lumbers off. I loft the ball farther to him,
and watch him juke and cut, old footwork,
the push between the knees and balls of feet.
The open north fence shows yellow farmland
we thought we'd all break free from
as easily as from a lineman's grasp. Now
in the slant light, my friend lines up, a man

like me past thirty. Something in the blood's
chill sends him running hard, pursuing
nothing but plain fact pulled down from
the sky. The ball whumps in his hands.
He dances, high-fives the air. Twilight
bends across his face as he trots back, turns
to line up again. "Go deep," I shout. "Go deep."

MY GRANDMOTHER VISITS

From her suitcase came a sigh of diesel
from stations, the breezy gust of arrivals
and departures. She'd settle in to her room,
then direct us down some stray, neglected highway—
hillsides, pastures, cows, hedgerows, hayfields.
Buckling exhausted houses. Acres of cottonfields

no different than when she'd gone down them
as a child, dragging a heavy bag. Glades fell open.
Each direction wrote its name, and whole histories
dropped out of the patchwork counties. Beside her,
I dreamed back the places she'd mentioned,
a scent of tobacco on her old breath. She'd sit

quiet for a moment, then spot some house
and start over: sumac, dogwood, sassafras. . . .
My father wheeled her past the stiles of fences,
taking first this direction then that, while
she breathed the shragged acres, and Back There
trundled behind us like a faithful wagon.

CROSSING THE COUNTRY ON AMTRAK

When I wake up, we're two states away, chuffing
up some hillside, lightning sudden profiling
some placeless weathered mountain in my window.
The old white bullet-headed porter's passing,
and the cars buffet and clank. Last night, boarding,
I climbed on and stumbled up the aisle, looking
for any seat among the sleeping bodies.
The train was pitching to one side and another,
lurching as we left the station. I stumbled
down the aisle, just hunting a place to fall.

There wasn't time to wave goodbye to my father,
outside on the platform, looking for me,
though as we pulled away I glanced out
in time to see him standing alone, searching
the windows, a quizzical smile crossing his face,
his hand upraised and frozen in a half-wave.
And though he didn't speak, I could still read him:
Son, I'd wave goodbye to you for sure
if I just knew where to find you. . . .

NIGHT ON THE BUFFALO

We rise to coffee, the amber day,
pitch our bags into the boats
and prepare to skim lucid gray water
toward rapids we heard all night,
whitewater coiling downstream,
singing through the crackling fire,
old stories weaving through the dark.

Something of us belonged
to ancient time, a breathing we left
by that hundred foot cliff heaved up
across the river from us, unseen.
All night I tossed in sleep,
the river's twists like fictions I dreamed,
bright knurls on the map.

Now we hear water, our anxious
hours scratched in lines on stone.
We drink coffee, hang our names
on limbs along the bank. The river's
voice slips through trees
and enters our hands.

MISSING CHAPTERS

Each year, diligent as a biographer,
my father seeks a war buddy, whom I know
from a blanched photo, and legend.
As if it were Patton's he pieces
the story together, though in India
the only bombs were locusts, the only sorties
mosquitoes' nightly runs. He picks up

the trail in Las Vegas, carries it
as far as Pennsylvania; describes the war
effort in Delhi: the tedium of parachute packers,
seasonal monsoons, how barracks shook at night
once during a quake. Dates and places
congeal around his friend, a man well-read
in Kipling, fluent in Hindustani, yet whose gift

for flatulence once impressed a whole platoon.
I try to enter that war, to know a soldier
whose heroic deed was to help my father survive
the boredom; whose life story vanishes
in the Sixties, amid the blackened
craters of bad marriage and alcohol—
the same cliche: a flier who bails out

in fog and is never heard from again.

FARM CLUB

The players take the field, a whole new nine,
uniforms aglow under April's sun,
the air washed with the scent of new-mown grass,
red dirt raked around the mound, bases,
home. The spraddled centerfielder thwaps twice
his fist in his glove, the umpire shoves
down his mask on his face then yells
and crouches behind the catcher, and the season's on.
In the stands, we're glad the perennial crank

has returned with his repertoire of taunts,
cliches and garbled one-liners he uses
not so much to annoy us as to maintain
the rhythm of the game in his own mind.
And now they're back, pitches blurring
from mound to plate, hanging curves, hard sliders,
bright streaks burned into the air, home runs
like rainbows whose far curves end beyond
these fences, in meadows like the ones
we crashed through as children, chasing this same light.

FLOUNDER FISHING NEAR THE REFINERIES

Fishing in the bay, just off the line
of oilrigs, we're close enough
to land to smell wet reeds, hear water
swish back and forth against the marsh,
yet close enough to the platforms
to hear the clang of steel, the putter
of engines pulling pure crude to the top.

Hardhats on break or loafing dawdle
and watch us, hang hands over the rail
and look down, daydreaming. Now and then
a copter buzzing the shore scares up
a pelican along the land. The waters
go swish, swish, gray-brown, sudsy,
a dirty froth riding small choppy caps

like heads on beer. The scent of oil's
in the air, clatter of industry, regular
chatter: someone's national hymn,
all metalwork and production. But what we
fish for flatten themselves along the slick
inlet bottom, look up, sometimes take hours
for bait we trawl before them like gold.

THIS MORNING SHE TALKED IN HER SLEEP

You turn into her speech as though it were
yours, as though you heard pure fear
spell itself and evaporate.
Once, as a boy, you watched letters form
nonsense in the thick alphabet soup.
It seemed futile then to try translating
that cryptic tongue. But here,
an hour before schoolchildren chatter past
your door with bright voices, and birds
on the awning create racket you can't ignore,

those hoarse sibilants spill out one by one
like notes you've been trying to write for months
in your mind to old friends who think
you'll forget them. Their wracked faces
wash up again and again in dreams you keep having.
Like jeering in a mirror, you're wild again,
they're yelling. Everything comes out backwards.

MAKING FLOWER POTS

Closing time at the plant, the presses clatter
to a stop, though the kilns go on baking
a thousand new pots to proper brick-like hardness.
The custodian pushes his broom along the center
and the foreman passes, whistling. Suddenly
the place is quiet. The roar is gone, the day's
dust still hanging, waiting to be rearranged again
tomorrow. Dormancy clamps down around
the bright planes and meditative presses
as night peeks in the broken windows above them.

We've wrapped today inside a box and sealed it
tight with an address. What soothes us
is the balm of sleep, dreams that arrive unbroken
and these small pools of quiet from which we'll sip
before tomorrow comes down again to stamp us
one shape, lift us up, ship us every direction.

SOUTHERN MALE NOVELIST

He comes along steeped in guns and bourbon,
whiskey-drinking, jon-boats, knife throwing,
the text a proving ground for manhood—
the story of a heavy-handed father who loved
but couldn't say or show it. Instead of
blasting small animals, he fires chapters, reams
of paper, at the dark. There's incest
in the family, and the wide swath of insanity.
His voice is the flat crack of a rifle.

CUCUMBERS

It's this way with me with cucumbers: pour a little
vinegar in a bowl, slice cucumbers into the vinegar,
sprinkle on a little black pepper, it's 1963. I'm nine
again, and the summer's erupting: the sun's high,
the days are long, and everything's coming in from
the garden: huge melons, tubs of corn, tomatoes,
crook-necked and white squash. Cucumbers sit on
the table in vinegar, in a bowl on the lazy susan;
Mother's in the kitchen stirring blackberry jelly, and
rumors abound of cousins due from far away later in
the week. There's the snap of summer crispness in
the air, and at night a full animal moon. When I look
in the mirror, I see vines for arms, leaves for hands,
and my face, suddenly turning green, moving toward
the light.

SUMMER RUN IN THE COUNTRY

The last car to pass you,
an hour ago, shook the primrose
and wild mustard along the road.
Now the sun tightens and glows
on stem and blade, bright
as a gun barrel. Rising heat
warps toward a thin blue sky
where thunderheads sprout
like popcorn. Nearer, the air
fills with the fierce hum
of insects hymning the season.
Worn from the pound of sneakers,
the scald of asphalt, you lean
against a post and try again
to think what mixture of vanity
and age drives you like an assassin
through July's sun blasting off
breathless trees, off horse
droppings toppled like stones
on the highway's yellow stripe.

KITE FESTIVAL

Today a hundred kites flap, bob and dart
around in air—one shaped like two legs, feet
and black pantaloons; one in a round whirly
multi-colored hurricane; one a great soccer ball.
Box kites, animal kites, even people loitering
holding makeshift kites made of yarn,
sticks, old plastic shopping bags! Each year
the kite show comes to town, and dutifully
the gods reply by sending one splendid blue
cloudless day with a full zephyrous wind—
this time from the north (usually it's
from the Gulf, full of moisture and warmth),
and with just a remnant of lingering winter chill.
There are kite ballets; the kids ride the jiggle bus;
people gnaw roasted weiners on a stick
and big hot corn ears pulled full-shuck from
a roaring oven. Dancers dance, singers sing;
whole families out in fields of knee-high grass
clutch small kites. The kites ride full wide
streams of air, up great billowing surges and drafts,
and soar popping diving swimming like
our days. And for a short time, we feel our lives
go slack, as if we could dance them on a string,
hurl them up there, let them flutter all day
to color the cold blue cloudless bolt of air.

DEALEY PLAZA

Stand here a moment:
brick walls all around, quiet traffic.
Look up at the window, down
at the street. Read the words.
This road's so narrow—how
could history have happened here?

Over there, the grassy knoll,
and something nearby, bigger
than anyone, higher than time
or a single moment. Here,
events came down so fast
a giant bridge from that day

still arches across, hooks onto
this one, holds the universe together.
You stand and look again.
A split second. The sun shines
hard, as it did that morning.
It breaks in your lashes.

FINGERPRINTS

The policeman slips into the official passive:
"entry was made through a back window."
He shows me the opened window, the frame
jimmied loose. He leads me through my own
house, writes on a yellow pad, then dusts
for fingerprints. Not much is missing,
but any unwanted entry's a violation.
"There's not much we can do," he says,
using this to segue into a sermon
I sense he has given often about how the legal
system's broken, how criminals can vault
right back out onto the streets too easily,
how parents no longer take responsibility
for their children, and so on. He scribbles down
his name and a case number on a card,
then hands it to me. "There's not much more
we can do now," he says, "we'll call if
something turns up." Then he climbs back
into his shiny copper-colored car,
and drives away, leaving me to go back
inside, to walk the halls alone behind
this dark presence suddenly in every room.
Closing at last the window where entry was made,
I see the floury black powder on the wall
and windows, still outlining and highlighting
the prints he found: etchings of some base need,
the black-purple coils and whorls a grimy
little signature, a handshake out of nowhere.

POISON

Here, they said, take this.
Dark and thick,
swung at me in a spoon,
a substance like pitch. I looked
and shook my head, No.
But why should you
be different, or difficult?
Here, they said.
No, I said, and balked.
They opened the records,
and sure enough: there
was the past. They showed me
the great machines,
the unmistakeable dark
markings of my own hands.
So, here, they said. Soon
you'll thank us. They smiled.
The spoon swung around again.
I opened my mouth.

II

THE UMBILICAL

for Chloe

After a day or two, it blackens
inside its clamp and protrudes
from her stomach hard and thick
as a small burnt stob of rope
or candle wick. Following the book's
instructions, I daub it with rubbing
alcohol, swash it back and forth
down to the point where it enters
her stomach. She squirms slightly,
or cries out when it stings. But
sometimes I stop and stare at it,
her only connection to the misty
other worlds. Were I to gain access
to her quickly receding recall
of that place, would my present
quandaries be solved? Did other souls
help her there to get here? Would I
recognize that world again myself
if I saw it? The blackness of
the drying blood cord suggests to me
the notorious quarrel
between flesh and spirit.
It reminds me of fresh mornings
when I was a child, kneeling
in the garden to see new melons
on their cords, an inch farther along
than they were the evening before
(I'd mark the place in dirt). Here,
there were mornings, still dark,
before she was born, when I would
awaken and hear her mother's faint,
sleep-leaden voice next to me

as she counted fetal kicks—*eleven . . .*
twelve . . . thirteen. Later,
I'd find the dim wobbly pencil lines
of her count she'd scraped down
in half-sleep on some torn-off
scrap of paper. Down that nine-
month corridor of our calmness
and periodic terror, our daughter
coursed, into this land. Now,
fresh and warm, wrapped up
like just-baked bread,
she quickly begins to fill into
her time. For a day or two,
I catch a brief unpleasant odor
of the dying flesh. Then,
one morning. half-looking while
thinking of something long ago
as I wash her, I realize the old
cord-stump has fallen away
somewhere, vanished.

CONTRARY

I think of her today, my long-deceased grandmother,
a hailstorm of a woman hulking and rumbling
through rooms, dragging her great stone unhappiness
up the years, the pinched gray bun on her head,
the doughy double chin, the voice a coarse mean bleat,
eyes drinking in all they didn't like—
measured cool gray eyes that didn't ask,
who has a place for us, the never satisfied?

She darkened where she went, and now her blood,
too, storms my veins, and I see how I've spent too many
days like this, fuming and blustering about
too little: money, time or energy. Nothing
won't task our reservoir of complaint.
Even the mildest day invites reproach.

ECLIPSE

Big wind in the trees, the moon's umber shape
in tossing shadows on the warm sidewalk.
You watch the shadows rotate—which way
will the world move tomorrow? Here you're held
by faith, a need to be in one place. The wind
whistles in treetops; the years mass,
break up and move away, your own
fixed planet occluded by this light.

You're no closer to knowledge than when the world
began. So soon the moon is gone, swallowed
by the world's murky forms. Clouded,
printed with self shapes, a dry empty air
breathing through, you want to learn
something, to make sense of what comes
and passes, but deep inside you know:
the faith you have may never be enough.

A DOOR AJAR

for HS

Waking in the room next to where you lay
facing an opened window, imagining afterlife—
thousands of acres of brilliantly lit poppies—
I hear syllables, scraps of talk, whispers
of a voice like yours. I didn't realize
I'd fallen asleep thinking of your long face,
the gaze you aimed one night right through me
at dinner. All through my nap today
a door ajar somewhere is bumping lightly.
Like a diver rising slowly to avoid the bends,
I surface fresh out of my deep dream:
acres of periwinkles, the ones it takes
a ton of to make a single cancer treatment.
In a light-washed room I crack my eyes to see
lace curtains lifting in April's rain wind,
to hear the banter of children and dogs outside,
and a door—bump, bump—an incessant message,
someone coming in, someone leaving.

SMALL LINES

You want to call it laughter, the sound water
makes rushing   rasping   running
over these flat stones, the creek quietly
braiding through a wide round turn near you,
crooking back through rocks, under yellow trees,
and out of sight. The creek crackles along,
ready to be moving—since motion is meaning—and
you watch and listen, held by all
that crinkles in the span of one day.

Later in the mirror you'll see lines
around your eyes, crimped places made by smiles
you've sent like cards to those who knew you. You lean
close and study them, such happiness
spread through years that crooked and braided
along. The sound comes closer, moves
around you like water quickening. Then, at once,
the lines bear in like marks cut in the stone—
you back away. The years go chuckling off.

THE FAMILY CRECHE

Each year in the cold dead winter, she'd think
how her father left, the sting of separation,
and she'd recall the manger scene the family hauled out
each Christmas to put on top of the mahogany
bureau, beside the chewed red candles,
the snowy paperweights, bells, cotton snowmen,
the gold-sprayed wreath made from Fortran cards
an aunt had furnished. She couldn't recall when,
but somewhere one year a wise man disappeared,

and then there were only two. Then another
vanished, and Joseph, and three lambs chipped.
Still each season, Mary looked down again,
and the Christ child was there. Her mother made them
put it all out each year, and on the bureau
they re-enacted in incompletion the pageant,
the blessed night, while over in its corner,
the spruce tree shrugged beneath its bent blue star.

PRESERVES

Wild plums bubbling and seething now cool in jars
on cabinet and counter. Front and back doors are opened,
and fresh air pours through, bringing scents of grass

and fresh-mown hay. Summer slows down to these
languid afternoons. Out the window, we see heat warp
off the road, making distance waver. One day last week,

we climbed and beat our way through grass and low limbs
to find the wild plum trees—a small grove, where buttons
bobbed red and yellow on spindly limbs. Our shoes dewy,

we stepped through picking quickly. July's morning sun
already hard on our faces, we dropped fruit in big tin cans,
the day heating up fast in snaky brambles and weeds.

Now that light, heat, fruit are stored in these quart jars
that line the kitchen, resting. Now and then, a jar lid,
remembering, sings it all back: *plink! plink! ploink!*

LEAP FAITH

for KD

When marriage went bad, she bailed out
to a new hobby, throwing herself
from a single-engine plane
to toll, bell-like, beneath a muslin
canopy, white as a wedding dress.

Gravity pulls her toward routine,
but she can hang suspended for now
above terrain checkered as a mother's
comforter. She can look down
on roofs and steeples, see all

in clear, antiseptic light, so high
no children call. The lure of invisibility
is clean as air, these miles
she's only seen from the weighted earth.
Dangling under silken lines,

in selfless abstraction, she treasures
each breath, each glimpse of bright,
uncluttered space, even as her world
reaches up, slips its knots around her ankles,
pulls her back.

TRIPLE A

The tiny radio mashed against my ear
barely bleeds through two drowsy batteries,
trickling into wee hours the manic clatter
and soul of our team's championship bash.
A hometown reporter's cornered Duncan
the catcher—two homers in the game
and the winning single—but he's modest
in afterglow, and doles the glory to all.
Not champagne but beer they pour atop
his head, against the slamming background
of lockers, whoops of teammates, the long
unwinding joy. All summer in upstairs heat
thick as a dog's pant, so dense some nights
I could barely lie still to listen, I heard
the season like some slow fever crest, coursing
along the rips and falls of fortune and rhythm.
Now, like the singular organism they are,
the players alternately laugh or step up to
the mike to break the season down to homily.
Their big voices booming all over town
find us in our beds, back yards, canneries,
warehouses, upstairs of stores, deep down
in the mines of our lives, the whir of voices
riding warm airwaves. Rapt, we listen
and breathe as around a fire, as summer
sags, dew-bespangled web, the long chill
fall soon to embrace us, one and all.

THE BOY IN THE DARK

Far off, heat lightning flickers on the horizon,
and the big May leaves are still. You turn over
in the iron-frame bed in your grandmother's house
to watch the storm far away, as old wood breathes
in the rafters, and the tin roof pops and settles.
Through the open window you can smell the garden;
already you can feel the world give up
its new warmth in a long meditated gush.
Tomorrows spill out of the ground toward you,

a future gaping wide as the sultry air that opens
to take you somewhere you don't know yet.
In this darkness, you feel trapped. Already
an energy's rising, an atmosphere gathering.
Somewhere else is spinning in the blood
its funnel. Soon it will swing down
into the days to come. Soon you'll explode,
and tear this long dark furrow across my life.

GOSSIP

In those old beauty salons downtown back home,
ladies with names like Bobette and Lavonne
still clip hair and talk pink talk about serial lives
they've heard tell of. *You don't mean that* and
Well I'd a never thought swirl down the sink
like clipped locks, phrases sighed from sticky
lips, smoke rings charming the soaped air.

Each day news walks in the front door afresh,
met by a bright bell and friendly hands
ready to take it. Soon, scrubbed, made over,
washed and pummeled, permed at last into myth,
it's sent back out, down the streets of home—
schools, bank, corner cafe, churches—
to become the things we know, what we all say.

AFTERNOONS IN THE COUNTRY CLUB

Old sterno cans arrayed across a table where
last night's dinner was served. The blonde woman
who tried to have me fired talking on the phone
behind the counter as I vacuum the floor,
bits of crackers scattered across the carpet.
Long silken cobwebs swaying off rafters,
too high to get to. Nostrils burn with ammonia
as I squeegee the top dormer windows clean.
Old rich golfers drag in from the course,
golf bags rattling. Cleats click and bony-thin
white legs stick out from checkered shorts
as they leave spike marks on the carpet. Cool air,
muzak moves in the empty spaces beneath
a vaulted ceiling, a calm and lazy feel here
late October afternoons, as bored bartenders
banter at their stations, setting up bottles
and glasses, another busy night coming.

LOSING MY WALLET

Even before I reached down to check—an instinct—,
I knew already: gone. A moment before,
I was swirling down a river of mall shoppers,
funneled along by Christmas, jostled and pushed
against a wall, carols breaking around us
like ornaments—such a power in the wallet,
a battery without which a man feels disconnected.
I turned and quickly tried to retrace my steps
past stores decked in holiday sausages, windows
with blouses, pre-faded jeans splayed in shapes
like the penniless. I broke into a run, pushed
my way past the Ear Piercing Boutique, the Silver
Shoppe, the Mean Bean Coffee Store, everywhere
encountering faces vaguely familiar, like ghosts
of Christmases past. At Santa's Castle,
I saw parents lined up and holding children,
each child cupping the small candle of want
in its eyes. I passed all the gifts yet unbought,
names of stores glossy as aluminum,
until at last I dropped down tired on a bench,
put my face in my hands and let fatigue come.
Closing my eyes, I could hear the steady tromp
of feet all around, until, drowsy, I could almost
make one set walk back, and recall the street-
corner years back where my father had opened
the car door and helped me inside, and I had sat,
as the heater purred, in the car's front seat,
watching as out the frost-webbed window
as he turned to go buy one last gift, strolling
back toward the dim line of stores
until the snow erased him.

FAMILY PROBLEMS

Back then, grownups sat up half the night talking,
going over family problems and oddities, avenues
where quandaries might lead. Over coffee, coke,
or tea, at the big wooden supper table, smoking
cigarettes, venting, our parents, grandparents,
uncles, aunts nursed their collective worries, while
we lay in bed, listening to quiet, measured talk
through walls, holding faith all would be resolved;

We knew our dreams would lift us up again, happy.
We knew time would come and tend patiently to all.
And sure enough, by morning all dishes were cleaned
and racked; all crumbs were swept off the table,
the chairs were scooted back up flush to the table's
wood; over a wall bar, the cup towel sat draped like a
resolution.

SULPHUR RIVER

It's olive drab and slow, hardly a river
this morning. I lean over the bridge:
two or three people perched below on buckets
drop their lines into the stinking roil
of current, a reeking pit slow as treacle,
creeping back far into the brambles,
places no one in his right mind would want
to wander, even at his most romantic.
Like a water moccasin, it slips off,
swirls by banks unknown, the blather of foam
and poison near some confluence with death.

Who but a mapmaker would want to follow
the dark current? I go no farther than here,
worries enough where I am to cloud the thoughts
as I hang my head over the metal railing
and mourn my nothings fiercely and long.
Below, my face waits pooling while I ride
in time these thoughts, tires singing
past, taking the bridges one by one.

LATE SEPTEMBER MOON

Round, full, it floats up over the eastern
treeline, rises orange and lonesome
over stubbled cornfields and the railroad tracks,
climbs bone-white into the high arch of the sky.
Sometimes at night, way out here in this
flat country, I stop on this road coming home
from work, and wait. The signal clangs,
the arm swings down, and the train's cars
pass clacketing by, with a breeze and leisurely
rhythm. I roll my window down: a breeze
scented like honey passes from the cool night
and I breathe in the acres like money.

The brown flatcars rock as they pass.
There's no one here, nowhere to go.
Nighttime's a quiet stretch, the moon's
silver sheen lathing down soundless
on all who wait. Then the last car passes,
the signal goes silent, the arm lifts again.
I go on, toward home, but part of me stays
forever back there with the luminous other
who floats, looking down on all, blessing
each of us with its quiet light.

THE LAST DOG

There'd been a string of eight or nine
in a row across the span of several years:
one dead of distemper; one hit
by our rural mailman's car; one strangled
by bigger dogs or coyotes in a field
near home; one simply vanished;
and one poisoned by a neighbor.
The last was an ugly, bloated
garlic-breathed Chihuahua mix,
which a friend, for some reason, gave us,
and which, because we could never think up
a name for it, my mother called "Mousey Turd."
It was small, chocolate brown, and we
took it out one winter morning to
the bad end of town, across the tracks.
I recall clearly: we drove down stark,
sad streets, past houses falling in, or
peeling paint, and some well-kept
but unlucky to be so close to the others.
We cruised blocks until we found
a spot reasonably inconspicuous,
then pulled to the curb, and opened
the door. There was no one out, no one
to be seen (it was Sunday morning),
and someone—Sister or I—nudged the dog
on the rear, and he stepped down on
the curb, one paw at a time, his ratty tail
curled between his legs. Then we closed
the door, and I looked out the back
windshield and watched him (it was
a cold morning; he looked afraid),
as my father turned and drove us back
up the street, whistling as he drove,
fiddling to find his favorite radio station.

THE WHEEL

As the ferris wheel was boarding, we felt it shake
till it stopped with us on top. With the girl I'd brought,
I gazed across the fairgrounds—colored lights, wheels,
the Haunted Castle, the slow amble of lovers around
     the Midway.

Farther, our town lay spread out—its darkened homes,
red and green traffic lights, its quiet buildings—
while cool air rode the September night. Beyond
lay the farmlands, our home, sheer blackness
where now and then a tiny light twinkled,
facets of a stone. Here, I thought,

we can all be held: this moment a wheel,
that poised and kept us. I breathed the cool air and waited.
Below us somewhere, at once, the engine coughed
and clattered, alive. The giant steel frame shuddered.
Swerving my last gaze outward, I looked once more
toward the night. Then the girl took my hand.
We started down.

LATE NIGHT RADIO

Glib talkers, weather reports
of blizzards and ice,
old hits from thirty years past
ride thousands of miles
across frozen continents
to my ears in the middle
of the night. Lying here

looking out the window
at fields in dead winter,
as my wife and kids
soundlessly sleep, I feel
I'm dialing up the dead,
or memory, a life
way in the past and gone.

If only I could reassemble
from it all the coherent world
of then, but it's all in these
bits and snatches now,
out of range, like far off
galaxies, wavery,
whistling, too far to pick up.

FISHING ON TOLEDO BEND

The summer sun anchors its weight to the lake,
bears down. It's hard not to feel crushed.
We trawl the inlet, toss hooks into clear, tea-colored
water, and wait. Our boat's finder shows schools
of fish beneath us: large commas with tails,
smaller specks. Nothing bites.

We move around, hugging shore, casting into
the tops of fallen pines. Someone's dumped
an ice chest on shore; we see the fenceline
go straight back to where the state owns
the land. And here's where the old county highway
crossed before they built the dam and buried
the roadway underwater. There's a steep, vertical

forty foot bank of iron-red East Texas soil,
over which the blacktop, still striped yellow,
juts out a few feet into space, and hangs there,
quiet, as we float by, as if someone one day,
driving along, distracted, flew straight off the end
into nothing, and kept going.

PANHANDLE

Perfectly square blocks.
Perfectly straight streets.
Perfectly right-angled
intersections. A land
flat as a tabletop.

Nothing so clear here
as a fact. Small houses
in broad plowed cottonfields
on the edge of town.
Ribbon highways where cars

hash past, going elsewhere.
Quiet, and distance, and space—
like this space I look across
northward, to the horizon,
where winter comes, blue as a knife.

SOMEWHERE IN AMERICA

Someone parked his rusted tractor in the pasture
behind the church and left it there years, as if he'd gotten off
and gone to the house for a drink, and would be back
any time, to finish the final patch of mowing. Mornings
after Sunday school, we'd run down to it, climb up
and around on it, shift its big gear shifter back, forth,
clank clank, while our parents visited in the church yard.

Remember that heavy sound? It filled us with a kind of
faith, belief in certainty, the grooved assurance of earth.
Some day we could go back and find it. Maybe it could tell us
where to go, point us to rows that are straight, buried
furrows that yield good crops. And it could sing into our
hands again the anthem of iron, when it drops into place
and carves truth deep into the fertile ground.

READING A DREAM

Sometimes I go back to an old house
and step into a room I've known;
there's a stillness that tends to all,
and the door opens as if nothing's changed.

But then I see that little ray of light
in one corner, or sense something new—
the color of paint, a potted plant
on the sill where we'd never placed one—

and I know: someone or many someones
have come and gone, and this room is time,
and it's never the same, and perhaps
I'm even dead, or so old I can't realize

how much has passed since I called
this room mine, when all the time
it wasn't. Part of me always resides
in these poised moments, places,

believing the lie time stands still,
as in a dream, that in each moment
I see poised, there's a date, a discovery,
something to leap out and save me.